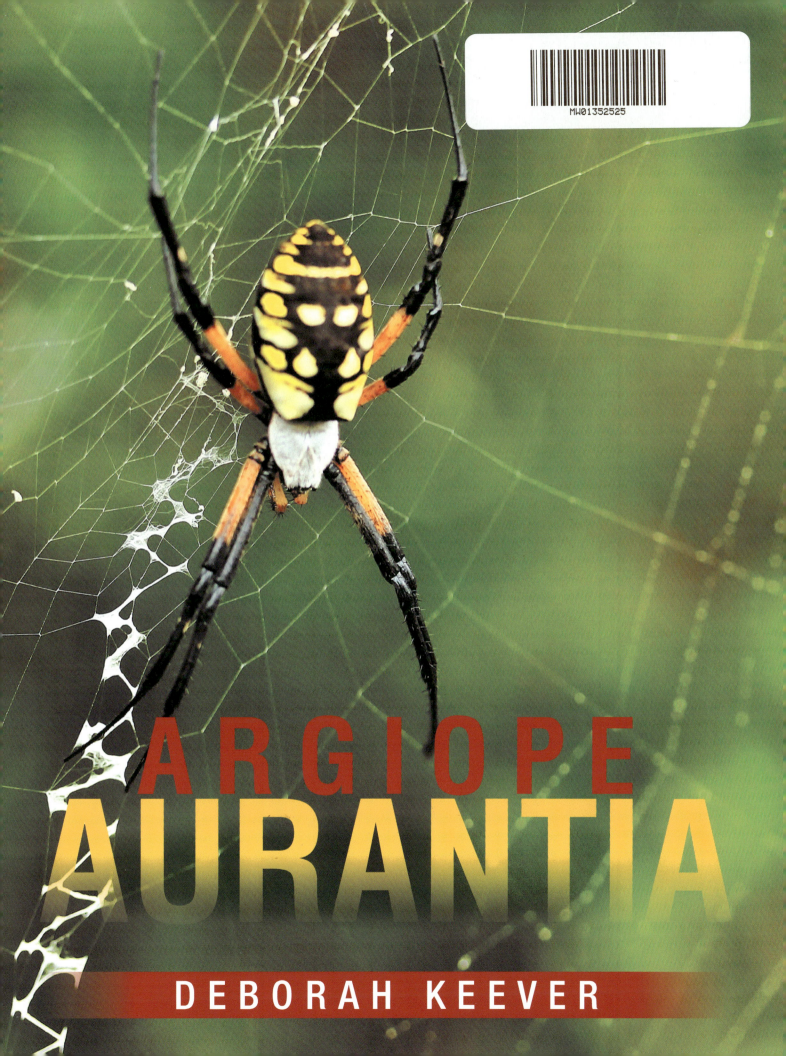

ARGIOPE AURANTIA

DEBORAH KEEVER

Copyright © 2014 by Deborah Keever. 696950
Library of Congress Control Number: 2014918829

ISBN: Softcover 978-1-4990-8564-8
EBook 978-1-4990-8563-1

All rights reserved. No part of this book may be reproduced or transmitted in any form or by any means, electronic or mechanical, including photocopying, recording, or by any information storage and retrieval system, without permission in writing from the copyright owner.

Rev. date: 10/22/2014

To order additional copies of this book, contact:
Xlibris
1-888-795-4274
www.Xlibris.com
Orders@Xlibris.com

Argiope Aurantia

Commonly called the Garden Spider, Writing Spider, Zipper Spider or Corn Spider.

Arachnophobia is the fear of spiders.

Arthropods belong to the largest order of Arachnids.

Argiope Aurantia is a invertebrated animal having an exoskeleton, a segmented body and joined appendages. Their legs are black with red or yellow bands on the segment nearest the body. Numerous black spines make up the legs.

Orb weavers, their webs look like a circle. Webs can be up to two feet diameters and are usually built after dark. They are hard to see because the silk is pure white.

The heavy zigzagging pattern found in their web is called "stabilimenta". Some say that it helps attract prey, some say that it keeps bigger animals out of the web and some think that it stabilizes the web. The stabilimenta reflect UV light.

The female usually sits in the middle of the web with her head down. She often keeps her legs close together so it looks as if she only has four legs.

A venomous bite paralyzes it's prey and helps to digest the prey's body. They can eat an insect twice their size. They mostly eat flying insects. They are harmless to humans.

Arachnids normally have two claw feet on each leg. Garden Spiders have three claw feet in order to handle the silk thread of the orb web.

She emits several stands of silk from her spinnerets that merge into one strand. The spinnerets is a red sac under her abdomen.

Their third pair of legs are much shorter than the other two. The short legs are located on either side of the head. They are very useful when spinning the web.

They lay their eggs in a egg sac in the Fall. They hatch but remain in the sac until Spring. Each sac contains between 400-4,000 babies They are surrounded in multiple layers of silk. Predators include ants, flying insects and birds.

The female is up to three times the size of a male. Females are 19-28mm or 3/4-1 1/8 inch log. Male are 5-9mm. Or ¼ -3/8 inch long.

Exoskeleton noted through the top part of the body appearing grey in color. Because the exoskeleton is hard young spiders must molt or shed their exoskeleton as they grow.

The Garden Spider

A giant black and yellow spider sits in her web
You can see her white furry head
The long jointed legs have a total of forty eight knees
So she moves over her web with great ease

Her prey sticks to the web with no chance of freedom
For the more they struggle, the more tangled they become
The spider is covered with oil so she will not stick
As she moves towards her prey for a quick prick

She quickly paralyzes her captive prey
And neatly wraps them in silk for a safe stay
Taking the prey back to the web's center
The Garden Spider will wait again in all her splendor

CPSIA information can be obtained at www.ICGtesting.com
Printed in the USA
BVIW12n1046070115
382141BV00004B/9